EMBRACING GRACE

Four bible studies about God's amazing grace with thoughtful reflections and things to do.

G. HOWARD MELLOR

ISBN 978 0 80671 827 7

Bible quotations are from the New Revised Standard Version.

British Library Cataloguing in Publication Data.

A catalogue record for this book is available from the British Library.

Dedication

To the Methodists of Hong Kong especially the congregations of the Methodist International Church whose lively faith, gracious hospitality and committed service were such an inspiration, and to Rosie for everything!

Acknowledgements

Even a short book like this needs all kinds of input to make it possible. Thanks are due to Methodist Evangelicals Together for having the courage to publish this book initially. Thanks too to Mr To Cok Sung of Lam Tin Methodist Church, Hong Kong who skilfully painted the bamboo images; to Martyn Atkins, Juli Wills and Rosie who read the text and offered wise comment; Anne Lim Chaplain for designing the book and to the team at Moorleys Print & Publishing Ltd for their attention to detail.

Above all, I am grateful to those many people who have taught me so much about and exemplified in their lives, God's grace. My prayer is that we all may continue to receive that grace and live it out to the full.

TABLE OF CONTENTS

Introduction:

Embracing Grace is a series of four bible studies about the Christian understanding of grace. The studies draw upon the Wesleyan understanding of grace and offer the material in an accessible and interactive format.

One of the gifts of the Wesleyan heritage to wider Christian thought is an understanding about the way God's grace is at work in our lives. It can be summed up in this way: Grace is God influencing and seeking (prevenient grace); God rescuing and redeeming (saving grace), God shaping and empowering (sanctifying grace) – so that we may be mature Christian people fitted for service. These are three ways of describing the mystery of God's grace, God's unconditional, unmerited, undeserved love for all humanity.

Bamboo is used here as a motif because bamboo is securely rooted, strong and yet flexible, always reaching skyward for light. In the right conditions it will grow a metre in a week. God's grace roots us firmly in Christ, to be strong in faith and flexible in witness, and of course to grow up into the fullness of the light and love of God. These studies explore the way we can be rooted in Christ and be embraced by the perfect love of God that we call grace.

You can use the material privately yourself or, even better, have enough copies to use with a small group. There are things to read, points to consider and opportunity to share and act.* Give it a go, and may God bless you!

G Howard Mellor

Revd Canon Dr G. Howard Mellor

Pentecost 2019

*the symbol indicates the points for reflection and action.

PREVENIENT
GRACE

Prevenient Grace

The Chinese have a wonderful story about a farmer who planted bamboo seed. The ground was good, moist and warm but in the first year nothing happened. Other plants flourished in the first year, and became more beautiful in the second year, but of the bamboo – nothing. The third and fourth year passed with nothing to show for the seed that was planted, and yet the farmer was patient. Then in the fifth year, the bamboo shoots appeared and grew up 80 feet in six weeks! God's grace is present and at work, before we ever know it. Such grace is at work in our lives quietly waiting for the moment when in the warmth of faith, it can grow. Sometimes it takes years, even decades, but it has been there all along.

God's grace is undeserved, is challenging, transforming and offered for all people. In these studies we are exploring grace from the perspective of prevenient, saving and sanctifying grace, one which, if received, shapes our lives.

We know the song and can hum the tune – *Amazing Grace*. But what about our experience of grace? For all of us there are moments when we begin to appreciate the notion that God is there for us.

- When were you first aware of being loved and nurtured by God or by anyone?
- Have there been moments when it has dawned on you that God cares for you and wants to nurture you?
- Did that realisation come early or has it been a recent experience?
- Or indeed is that awareness of being loved a difficult concept for you?

Let us be clear, grace is all about God. It is God's gift for us, undeserved, unlimited and free! For all of us there are moments when we are aware of the presence of the divine, often not anywhere near a church, when we realise God is nudging us by his presence in our lives. The seed of grace planted in our lives.

We are adding a word in this study, *Prevenient* - a word which is not in common use so let us explore it. Prevenient – literally means – coming before – to anticipate, to be expectant. Prevenient refers to the undeserved love of God which runs ahead of us. It also has a lesser known meaning to 'prevent waywardness, guard against evil'.

Prevenient grace is a way of saying that there is a moment in the lives of most people when we come to the realization that God has been looking out for us. If you like - God has been knocking at the door of our lives.

Look at this Psalm and think about how it relates to your life:

O Lord, you have searched me and known me.

You know when I sit down and when I rise up;

you discern my thoughts from far away.

You search out my path and my lying down,

and are acquainted with all my ways. ...

For it was you who formed my inward parts;

you knit me together in my mother's womb.

I praise you, for I am fearfully and wonderfully made.

Wonderful are your works; that I know very well.

My frame was not hidden from you,

when I was being made in secret,

intricately woven in the depths of the earth.

Psalm 139:1-3; 13-15

Are there parts of your life or faith journey you can share with people in your group? How do you respond to the psalm? You could also look at the other texts below and see which resonate with you.

- 'Before I formed you in the womb I knew you, and before you were born I consecrated you...' Jeremiah 1:5
- '...I have loved you with an everlasting love: therefore I have continued my faithfulness to you.' Jeremiah 31:3
- 'For thus says the Lord GOD: I myself will search for my sheep, and will seek them out...I will seek the lost, and I will bring back the strayed, and I will bind up the injured, and I will strengthen the weak... I will feed them with justice.' Ezekiel 34:11, 16
- 'For the Son of Man came to seek out and to save the lost.' Luke 19:10
- 'And I, when I am lifted up from the earth, will draw all people to myself.' John 12:32
- 'Do you not realize that God's kindness is meant to lead you to repentance.' Romans 2:4
- 'We love (God), because he first loved us.' 1 John 4:19
- 'For God so loved the world that he gave his only Son, so that everyone who believes in him may not perish but may have eternal life. Indeed, God did not send the Son into the world to condemn the world, but in order that the world might be saved through him.' John 3:16-17

Exploring Wesley

Methodist Christians believe that we cannot simply know God by reasoning alone but we also need to experience God in a personal way. This comes from the experience of our founder John Wesley, who for years sought to gain God's favour through pious actions such as attending worship, prayer, reading scripture. On the 24 May 1738, it dawned on him that God's grace was freely available for him. He wrote in his Journal:

In the evening I went very unwillingly to a society in Aldersgate Street where one was reading Luther's preface to the Epistle to the Romans. About a quarter before nine, while he was describing the change which God works in the heart through faith in Christ, I felt my heart strangely warmed. I felt I did trust in Christ, in Christ alone for my salvation; and an assurance was given me, that he had taken away my sins, even mine, and saved me from the law of sin and death.

This experience of God's grace changed his life and ministry. Wesley was assured of saving grace and later reflected on the way God had been working in his life. He wrote about what he called 'prevenient grace' by which he meant that God graciously seeks out people and calls them from sin, recalling them to faith in Jesus. In his sermon *On Working Out Our Own Salvation,* he wrote that prevenient grace encouraged 'the first wish to please God, the first dawn of light concerning his will' (Sermon 85).

Wesley also wrote about 'convincing grace' which leads to repentance. Mark's gospel opens with the call of Jesus to repentance ('Repent and believe the Good News', Mark 1:15), literally, to turn around, to turn away from sin and turn towards the transforming love of God.

Throughout Wesley's account of prevenient grace there is the image of God knocking on the door of people's lives, wooing them to consider seriously the claims of Jesus. Everyone could receive this grace and no-one was excluded. He knew from his own experience, and saw in the lives of his early preachers, that God's grace was at work in their lives before ever they realised it.

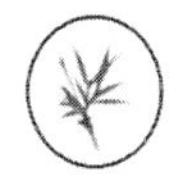

If you had to draw a line representing your faith journey so far – how would it look? Take a moment to draw that journey on a clean page using what colours suit your journey. Is it straight, or up and down or whirling around? If you are in a group you may choose to share what you have drawn.

Exploring Scripture

Being aware of the Methodist emphasis, we need now to explore what the Bible says about God and God's grace. Prevenient Grace is God's activity in calling us from the moment of our conception into a loving relationship with God. Such grace reveals God's deep desire that everyone is able to respond to God's offer of love. Grace is the divine love that God has for us: grace lived out by Jesus, John 1:16; grace as a gift, Romans 3:24; grace which is sufficient for all our needs, 2 Corinthians 12:9.

We see the grace of God in the lives of characters in the Bible. The following four people emerge on the stage of the biblical record and every one of them has a back story of seeking before we read about them.

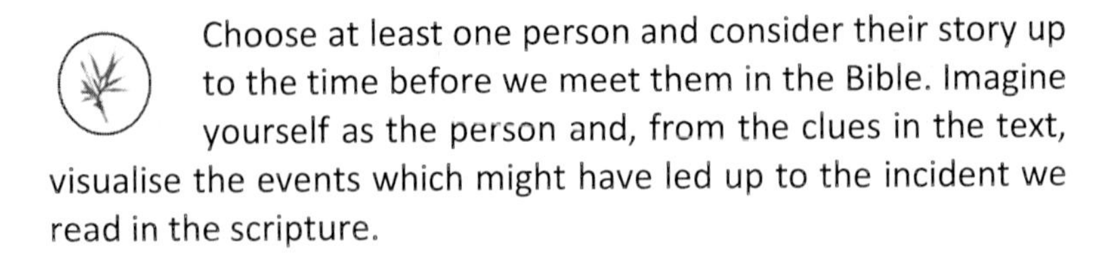

Choose at least one person and consider their story up to the time before we meet them in the Bible. Imagine yourself as the person and, from the clues in the text, visualise the events which might have led up to the incident we read in the scripture.

Lydia, a merchant in expensive fabrics who was a 'worshipper of God' which made her ready to 'listen eagerly' to the good news of Jesus (Acts 16:12-15).

Zacchaeus, a disliked tax collector who climbed a tree to satisfy his curiosity to see Jesus, who he heard had changed lives. Is there, in his curiosity, a desire and longing for a transformed life? (Luke 19:1-10).

Nicodemus, a learned leader in Jerusalem who had questions to explore and came in the evening gloom seeking answers (John 3:1-10 and 16-17).

The woman by the well, whose name curiously we do not know, but about whose life much is revealed. She comes to the well in the midday heat, possibly to avoid others drawing water in the cool of the day. Her conversation with Jesus reveals she has thought a great deal about worship. The effect of her response to Jesus had a dramatic effect in her community (John 4:1-42).

How do you relate to your chosen character – what do they teach you about God's grace?

Prevenient Grace is about a Seeking God

The Bible speaks of the seeking love of God, who takes the divine initiative in the relationship and pursues us throughout our lives.

- God calls us even before we are born - Psalm 139, Isaiah 49:1.
- God walks with us through all our days - Psalm 23:6, John 1:47-49.

The heart of the good news is that God has taken the initiative to seek and to save the lost (Luke 19:10). God is not waiting for people to come to him, God is seeking them out. Luke sets this great truth in three parables in Luke 15. Jesus has been criticised about mixing with sinners (15:1-2). He replies with three parables in which there is a search - for the sheep that has strayed, the coin that has been misplaced and finally, he speaks of the son who has turned his back on the family. The central character in what we call the parable of the prodigal son is in fact the 'longing, loving Father' who runs to meet the son, illustrating the seeking love and grace of God.

Prevenient Grace is about an Inviting God

When Jesus sees Zacchaeus up the tree in Jericho, he knows him by name (Luke 19:5). Jesus' call to repentance was a call to respond to the divine invitation. Repentance is itself a gift (convincing grace), the opportunity to turn towards God. The emphasis is not on forsaking sin but rather is on receiving the offer of God's transforming love. God is seeking out people and inviting them to embrace God's love. Such grace seeks to bring us into a relationship with God – so we are invited to call God '*abba*', Father. Note that 'Father' here is not about gender as though God is male but about the intimacy of the parent-child relationship. We may whisper *abba* with confidence that God hears our prayer.

Prevenient Grace is about a Transforming God

God's love in Christ is certainly 'seeking love' but also 'holy love'. The grace of God which comes to us, challenges our lives, and begins the process of transforming us. Prevenient grace is a way of saying that the grace of God comes before we ever know it and as we respond, God is changing and transforming our lives, shaping our values and behaviour.

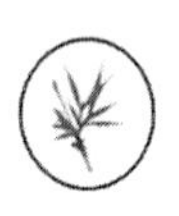

At the heart of the Methodist service of baptism we have a declaration which captures the thought of prevenient grace. The early prayers all speak of the grace of God and then the minister says to the one about to be baptised, whether adult or small child – who of course will probably not understand what is being said to them, though that only strengthens the point:

> *(Your name),*
>
> for you Jesus Christ came into the world;
> for you he lived and showed God's love;
> for you he suffered death on the Cross;
> for you he triumphed over death,
> rising to newness of life;
> for you he prays at God's right hand:
> **all this for you,**
> before you could know anything of it.
> In your Baptism,
> the word of Scripture is fulfilled:
> 'We love, because God first loved us.'
> (Methodist Worship Book, pp. 92-93)

Read this prayer using your own name in the first line. How does this prayer reflect your experience of God?

Pray and Act:

We have an opportunity to give thanks to God. There is an image of a flower (see page 13), which you could copy and enlarge. Cut out the flower and in the centre of the flower write the things for which you wish to give thanks. Colour the petals as you reflect on the way God has revealed himself to you. Fold the petals inwards along the dotted line.

Then place the flower/s on a tray or shallow bowl of water. As you watch the prayer petals open up before God, say a prayer of thanksgiving. Perhaps use this prayer:

> The Lord bless you and keep you;
> the Lord make his face to shine upon you
> and be gracious unto you;
> the Lord lift up his countenance upon you
> and give you peace. Amen.

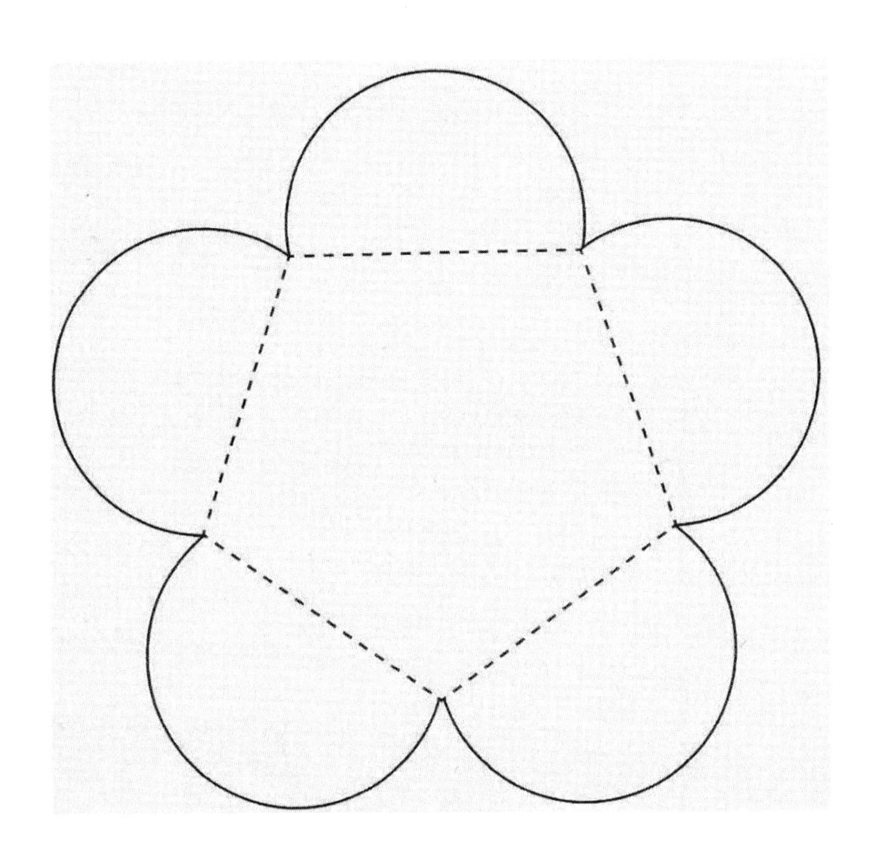

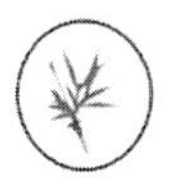

Methodism was 'born in song'. Charles Wesley wrote many thousands of hymns so that people could learn and understand their faith by singing. Read this hymn. If you were to place one verse in your purse or wallet, or as a fridge magnet, which would it be?

O for a thousand tongues to sing
my great Redeemer's praise,
the glories of my God and King,
the triumphs of his grace!

My gracious Master and my God,
assist me to proclaim,
to spread through all the earth abroad
the honours of your name.

Jesus! the name that charms our fears,
that bids our sorrows cease,
'tis music in the sinner's ears,
'tis life, and health, and peace.

He breaks the power of cancelled sin,
he sets the prisoner free;
his blood can make the foulest clean;
his blood availed for me.

See all your sins on Jesus laid:
the Lamb of God was slain;
his soul was once an offering made
that all may heaven gain.

In Christ, our Head, you then shall know,
shall feel your sins forgiven,
anticipate your heaven below,
and own that love is heaven.

Charles Wesley

SAVING
GRACE

Saving Grace

God's saving grace is wonderful. In 635AD when the Chinese Emperor T'ai-tsung heard the message of God's salvation from the Syrian monk Alopen he declared, 'it is mysterious, wonderful, spontaneous, producing perception, enabling essentials for the salvation of creatures and the benefit of man. It ought to spread throughout the Empire.' He endorsed what he called this 'luminous religion' (from the Chinese 景教, meaning 'luminous', 'illustrious', 'brilliant' teaching).

This card was produced by Trappist chocolate makers in S. France. Each box had a collectable card and one depicts Alopen declaring the Christian message to the Emperor. Note: the French Catholics spell his name Olopen.

Christianity came to China in the same year that Aidan came from Iona to convert the English. Which of T'ai-tsung's words strike a resonance with you?

Wesley on Saving Grace

Salvation, according to John Wesley had 'two grand branches' – justification and sanctification. By justification we are saved from the guilt of sin, and restored to the favour of God. By sanctification we are saved from the power of sin and restored to the image of God. In this section we are exploring God's saving, justifying grace.

In his sermon 'Free Grace' Wesley speaks of God's undeserved and free flowing love for humanity, 'The grace or love of God, whence cometh our salvation, is FREE IN ALL, and FREE FOR ALL' (Sermon 128, the capitals are his). It is not only free but also universal. All may come in every place and for all time.

By free 'in all' Wesley means that it does not depend on the ability of people, but rather salvation flows from the 'free grace of God'. God's grace is 'for all.' There is not one person who has lived for whom God's grace has not been offered. Jesus Christ was, according to Wesley, 'full of grace and truth and while on earth he spoke everywhere as if he were willing that all should be saved. To say, then, he (i.e. God) did not intend to save all sinners, is to represent him as a gross deceiver of the people.'

We need saving grace because 'all have sinned and fallen short of the glory of God' (Romans 3:23). Wesley referred to the sin which affects us all as a 'loathsome leprosy'. He would say to his hearers, 'know your disease' and then point them to Jesus to 'know your cure'. What Wesley called Saving or Justifying Grace describes the work of Jesus Christ on the cross for us. God offers mercy and forgiveness to all who come penitent, desiring to know and serve God. The life, death and resurrection of Jesus had made salvation available to all people in every place and for all time.

Saving grace is the good news that God in Jesus offers salvation to all who come to him. We cannot earn saving grace – it is to be received. We take hold of saving grace when we realise that we do not merit the relationship with God, it is not something we work our way into. God has already accepted us – already Jesus has died and risen for us – saving grace has been there all our lives. It is experienced when we accept the relationship that is offered to us, when we understand that God accepts us just as we are. When we realise we are embraced by God's grace.

Saving grace needs our response, our turning around, our awakened awareness, eyes opened to the love and companionship of God, saying 'yes' to God's offer through true repentance and amendment of life. Wesley writes:

You can do something, through Christ strengthening you. Stir up the spark of grace which is now in you, and he will give you more grace...You must be 'workers together with him' (Philippians 2:12 – 'work out your own salvation with fear and trembling').

The Friday we call 'Good'

Good Friday is a tough story. It is about the scandal of a popular hero tricked by the authorities, tried on fabricated charges and given a cruel death. It is a story which we have abandoned, in contemporary imagery, in favour of bunnies, chocolate and chicks. Here it is:

Jesus had been on the way to Jerusalem for some time. His closest friends tried but did not really understand his main purpose in coming. On the day we call Palm Sunday Jesus came from the villages of Bethany and Bethpage with those friends into Jerusalem riding on a donkey. It signalled he came in peace, and the crowd welcomed him into the city. That week the authorities tried to catch Jesus out with questions in an attempt to trick him into offending the Roman or the religious authorities. They wanted an excuse to arrest him.

On Thursday Jesus had a meal with his disciples. He washed their feet and after the meal they shared bread and wine. Jesus went, as he often did, to the shady olive grove in the garden of Gethsemane, where he prayed. Here under cover of darkness Judas led the soldiers to find him.

Jesus was quickly brought before three courts: the Jewish leaders, to Herod at his Palace, and before Pilate. Witnesses were brought but no accusation stuck. Finally, before an early morning crowd Pilate offered to release a prisoner and suggested Jesus. But the crowd shouted 'Crucify him!' Pilate agreed unwillingly and washed his hands of the situation. Jesus was, at Pilate's orders, whipped and stripped. Jesus, tied to a cross beam, stumbled his way through the city and up the hill outside the city. There on the hill called Golgotha he was crucified with two criminals. Most disciples fled, his opponents jeered, soldiers threw dice for his clothes. His mother, Mary, other women and John were there. Many others witnessed this event. Jesus cried out in agony and died.

The women and a rich friend, Joseph, took down his body, wrapped it carefully and placed it in a tomb. Nothing happened on the Saturday, the Sabbath. Early on the Sunday morning the women came to place spices and herbs with the body. In the mist they saw someone whom they assumed to be the gardener. The resonance of his voice told them this was Jesus - the tomb was empty. Jesus appeared to the women first, then the amazed disciples. He is Risen! Three words that changed their world.

Imagine the scene

To help in thinking about this event. Take a cross (or three crosses), and make a simple 'hill' of cloth or card. Imagine this is the scene outside Jerusalem and place the cross/es on the hill and the empty tomb nearby. We know from the gospel record some of the people and groups who were there. On pieces of card write their names: Mary, Other women, John, Soldiers, Other disciples, Two criminals, Centurion, Scoffers, Scribes, Pharisees, Priests, Simon of Cyrene, Joseph of Arimathea, Jesus. Place them at the scene you have made.

Where do you think the people were? Are they near the cross or far away? Are they drawing closer or backing off? As you place them, think about how the different characters might feel?

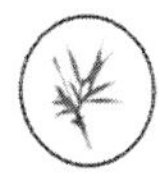

From what you know of the Easter story:

- Who would you be?
- Where would you be standing?
- What would you be feeling?
- If you had something to say what would it be?
- Think about the way the scene changes as the women discover the empty tomb on Easter Day.

Understanding Saving Grace

What are the words and images you would use to describe a rescue? For instance – a lifeboat is there to 'save' those who are in danger on the sea.

When we think about the difference Jesus makes through the cross and resurrection we are speaking of the most incredible mystery. The glorious mystery that God in Christ dies for us, and in his person takes on all the suffering and hurt and pain and sin, of all people in every place and for all time. God comes to rescue and liberate us that we may be the people he wants us to be.

The writers of the New Testament used four images as they sought to convey in words what they believed to be the truth about the death and resurrection of Jesus. They were seeking to describe the difference Jesus makes for us.

1. Practice in the Temple

The image here is of the sacrificial system of the temple in which there is a sacrifice for sin. There is a word, *hilasmos*, which we find in 1 John 2:2; 4:10; Romans 3:25; Hebrews 2:17; Luke 18:13. In more recent versions of the English Bible the word is translated using the phrase 'atoning sacrifice'. *Hilasmos* is a word which has two strands of meaning relating to the death of Jesus on the cross: one indicates that God's love opens up a way for us, another conveys that the wrath of God is turned away from us.

These writers are seeking to convey that God in Christ dies on the cross for us. His sacrifice deals with sin, once and for all. God does not love us because Christ died for us, Christ died for us because God loves us. In this sense the death of Jesus was God's perfect gift to make a way for us.

2. Transactions in the Market Place

The image here is brought to us by the word *lutroo* meaning 'to redeem'. It is a technical term and appears in Mark 10:45 and was used of buying back, setting free. In the Old Testament, property, animals, persons and even a nation can be set free. Mark 10:45 and 1 Timothy 2:5-6 contain this idea of ransom.

Ransom is also about liberation. There are many images within the Bible, which speak of liberation, not least Moses and the children of Israel, or people Jesus dealt with such as Zacchaeus, or the woman at the well. Jesus is our liberator, setting us free from sin enabling us to 'walk in newness of life' (Romans 6:4). By this 'ransom' the holy love of God comes to set us free from personal and structural sin; to help us become the very people God wants us to be.

3. Judgment in the Law Court

The image here is of the courtroom. The person before the judge is found guilty, but having pronounced judgment the judge comes to take the prisoners place. They are *dikaiothentes* 'justified' (Romans 5:1). When we come to God asking for forgiveness the grace of God intervenes to forgive, to wipe the slate clean. It is time for us to make a new start and receive God's lavish grace in our lives. The judgement we should receive, God in Christ gladly takes and sets us free. We are justified and can know peace with God. Then it is time to show a changed life!

4. Relationships in the Home

The image here is of the home with family and friends and in particular our relationship with God (Romans 5:10). The focus is one of reconciliation in which 'in Christ, God was reconciling (*katallanssōn*), the world to himself' (2 Corinthians 5:19). What is offered is a new relationship with God in which we may talk to him using the intimate term, *abba*. The response of faith to the grace of God means that we are 'adopted' into the family of Christ (John 1:12-13; Ephesians 1:5; 1 John 3:1-10). To be reconciled with Christ (Ephesians 2: 17-18), is to come within the orbit of his challenging and transforming holy love.

A new relationship with God means a new relationship with the people of God (Ephesians 2:11-22). Racism and sexism are challenged, status is irrelevant among the reconciled people of God. Indeed, there is a new relationship with all things (Colossians 1:15-20). God in Christ comes to reconcile the whole cosmos, which has been ruptured by sin.

Your Journey of Faith

Think about your journey of faith so far. How do you think about it and what words do you use?

In the diagram below are words which are often used. Is there one to which you relate most strongly – or do you choose a cluster of words?

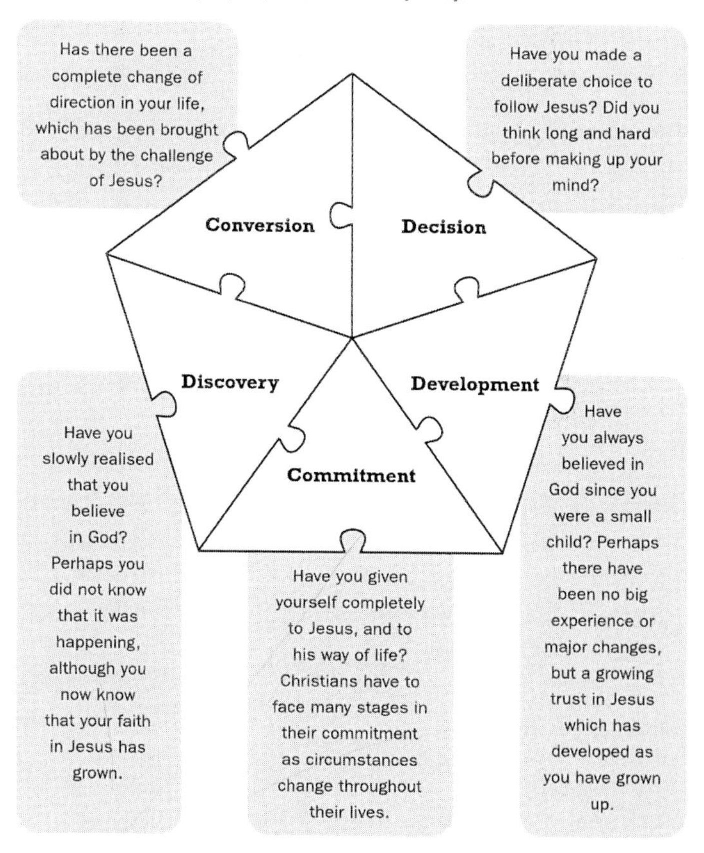

Now return to the four New Testament images: Practice in the temple, Transactions in the market place, Judgement in the law court, Relationships in the home. Consider how you relate to them, and why?

Key Bible verses

Mark 1:15

Repent and believe the good news!

Mark 10:45

For the son of Man came not to be served but to serve, and give his life a ransom for many.

John 10.10

I came that they may have life, and have it abundantly.

Matthew 11:28

Come to me, all you that are weary and are carrying heavy burdens, and I will give you rest. Take my yoke upon you, and learn from me; for I am gentle and humble in heart, and you will find rest for your souls. My yoke is easy, and my burden is light.

Ephesians 2:4-5, 8-10

But God, who is rich in mercy, out of the great love with which he loved us even when we were dead through our trespasses, made us alive together with Christ—by grace you have been saved...For by grace you have been saved through faith, and this is not your own doing; it is the gift of God not the result of works, so that no one may boast. For we are what he has made us, created in Christ Jesus for good works, which God prepared.

2 Corinthians 5:17-19.

So if anyone is in Christ, there is a new creation: everything old has passed away; see, everything has become new! All this is from God, who reconciled us to himself through Christ, and has given us the ministry of reconciliation; that is, **in Christ God was reconciling the world to himself**, not counting their trespasses against them, and entrusting the message of reconciliation to us.

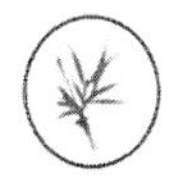

Look at the Bible passages.

- Read them through thoughtfully.
- Now read them again and this time underline or highlight passages.
- What is it that God wants to offer us?
- What does God in Christ do for us?
- What do these passages suggest we should do?

A meditation to use in your prayers:

Atonement

Jesus dies,
exposed and alone.
The one on whom we pinned our hopes
is nailed to the cruel tree.
On this Friday, we call *Good*
scheming leaders manipulate power,
pass the buck, wash their hands.
Jesus, stripped and whipped,
strapped beneath a cross beam
stumbles upward
radiating mercy.

On this tree,
plain and stark
encrusted with sin,
sparkling with love,
the nailed God
offers mercy and forgiveness.
A new beginning for all
who come, humbly and penitent,
seeking grace,
desiring to walk
in newness of life.

Here is another well-known hymn by Charles Wesley which conveys the joy of salvation. Is there a phrase in the hymn you find particularly helpful?

And can it be that I should gain
an interest in the Saviour's blood!
Died he for me? who caused his pain!
For me? who him to death pursued?
Amazing love! How can it be
that thou, my God, shouldst die for me?

'Tis mystery all: th' Immortal dies!
Who can explore his strange design?
In vain the firstborn seraph tries
to sound the depths of love divine.
'Tis mercy all! Let earth adore;
let angel minds inquire no more.

He left his Father's throne above
(so free, so infinite his grace!),
emptied himself of all but love,
and bled for Adam's helpless race.
'Tis mercy all, immense and free,
for O my God, it found out me!

Long my imprisoned spirit lay,
fast bound in sin and nature's night;
thine eye diffused a quickening ray;
I woke, the dungeon flamed with light;
my chains fell off, my heart was free,
I rose, went forth, and followed thee.

No condemnation now I dread;
Jesus, and all in him, is mine;
alive in him, my living Head,
and clothed in righteousness divine,
bold I approach th' eternal throne,
and claim the crown, through Christ my own.

Charles Wesley

SANCTIFYING GRACE

Sanctifying Grace

We normally assume 'perfect' to refer to something, or someone, who is not deficient in any way, unblemished, faultless, pristine. Often the people or items are lavish, expensive, aloof.

As we shall see the bible uses 'perfect' in a different sense – as of something or someone who has returned to God and is restored, perfected.

I live in Winchester where there is a magnificent Cathedral. It has a huge west window in the nave which could be described as beautiful, but it is not pristine. In 1642, during the English Civil War, Oliver Cromwell's soldiers overran Winchester. They ransacked the cathedral and, with muskets, shot out the coloured glass saints of the huge west windows. Under cover of dark, local people gathered up what they could of the shattered glass and carefully hid it for eighteen years.

When peace returned in 1660 the glass was put back, but not as it had been. It was carefully restored but with the glass pieces placed randomly in a mosaic. The scarred cathedral window was lovingly reshaped into something stunningly beautiful – a different kind of perfect.

We may be people who are scarred, damaged, broken, but when God reshapes us by his sanctifying grace we are transformed, restored, complete – made perfect in a different way.

Looking at Scripture

If we look at the New Testament we discover there are two groups of words which are translated 'perfect', *Teleios* and *Katartizō*

Ephesians 4:13 - Teleios – referring to the goal of Christian discipleship – maturity in Christ. The word refers to: being complete, mature; to make perfect by reaching an intended goal; a full complement of sailors on a ship; to bring to a full end.

John 17:23 - Jesus' prayer that we would be *completely* one – so that...

Matthew 5:48 - being mature and *complete* as is your heavenly Father.

Colossians 4:12 - behaving in a *mature* way, toward outsiders.

Matthew 4:21 - Katartizō - referring to the mending of nets and is often used in practical ways such repair, fit, frame, mend, restore, complete.

1 Corinthians 1:10 - *restored* believers who are of the same mind and judgement.

Galatians 6:1 - call to *restore* other Christians, in a spirit of gentleness.

Colossians 3:14 - made to be in *harmony* with God and each other.

1 Thessalonians 3:10 - to supply or *complete* what is lacking.

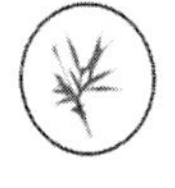

Look at the texts for *Teleios* and *Katartizō* and consider what they say to you. How do they suggest the people or situations are perfect? How do they suggest the people written to are on a journey to being reshaped by grace?

Sanctifying Grace Shapes our Lives

God fills us with his love so that, in the power of the Holy Spirit, we may express outwardly the life of Christ in our lives. Sanctifying grace is dynamic. It is life-transforming and introduces a radical difference to us – a life that has quality. This is not an experience intended for personal consumption and personal delight. It is to be shared.

The letter to Christians in Ephesus exhorts them to express the life of Christ:

- Ephesians 2:10 – salvation is by faith and through grace but we are created for 'good works'.
- Ephesians 4:22-24 - putting off (putting away) and putting on (clothe yourself) – the language of baptism in which the person being baptised cast off their old cloak, was baptised and then put on a new cloak worn for the

first time. It was a symbol of putting off the old life and taking hold of a new way of living.

- Ephesians 4:23 - receiving God's grace is a deliberate act of will, an attitude of the mind which affects behaviour, values, relationships.
- Ephesians 5:1 - 'be imitators of God' – being a mirror image of Christ. This is why the fruit of the Spirit are so important because together they are the expression of the life God brings to our lives by the power of the Holy Spirit.
- Ephesians 5:3 – God's grace affects all our relationships with others; highlights the importance of close relationships and the way we treat others. Such grace encourages us to love others as Christ would do.

If you were to describe a person who 'Expressed Christ' in their lives - what would you expect to see? What sort of evidence would you find in their lives?

How does this Work?

Spiritual experience has long been understood to be both gradual and instantaneous. People may speak of a 'sudden' realisation but usually when they reflect on it they realise God has been at work in their lives for some time! Moments of sudden disclosure are normally preceded and followed by the work of God's Holy Spirit moulding and shaping our lives. We noted that when considering Saving Grace. Look again at the jigsaw diagram on p.25. What words would you choose to describe your personal and spiritual journey now?

Wesley on Sanctifying Grace

Throughout his ministry John Wesley spoke of sanctifying grace. His reading of scripture led him to believe that the person who finds faith in Christ is filled with the love of Christ. This divine love, he argued, would bring them maturity, to be 'perfect'. He urged people to long for, to pray for, the perfect love of Christ to fill their lives by the power of the Holy Spirit.

The doctrine was discussed at the first Methodist Conference in 1744 where the question (set by Wesley) was raised, 'What is implied in being a perfect Christian?' The answer given (by Wesley) was, 'loving the Lord our God with all our heart, and with all our mind, and soul, and strength (Deuteronomy 6:5; 30:6; Ezekiel 36: 25-9)'.

In a letter to Hannah Ball, a pioneer of Methodist Sunday Schools, Wesley wrote, 'All that is necessarily implied therein (in Christian Perfection), is humble, gentle, patient love, love regulating all the tempers and governing all the words and actions' (Letters, Vol 6, p.65).

Wesley commented on the use of the word 'perfect' in the letter to the Hebrews (Hebrews 10:14; 11:40; 12:23): 'But what is perfection? The word has various senses: here it means perfect love. It is love excluding sin; love filling the heart, taking up the whole capacity of the same' ('The Scripture way of Salvation',1765, *Sermon 43).*

Wesley makes the same emphasis in a letter to Walter Churchey in 1771: 'Entire sanctification, or Christian perfection, is neither more nor less than pure love - love expelling sin and governing both the heart and life of a child of God' (*Letters*, Vol.5, p.223).

So, for Wesley, sanctifying grace, or Christian perfection, is the operation of God's love in the life of the Christian in such a way that the love of God is fully alive in us. Therefore 'Love' – 'pure love' – 'love expelling sin' – 'perfect love': these were the descriptions, which Wesley employed to express the heart of what he meant.

Wesley considered the question of whether sanctification or holiness occurs suddenly in a crisis experience, or as a maturing process. To one of his preachers, George Gibbon, he wrote, 'It is our duty strongly and explicitly to exhort the believers to go on to perfection, and encourage them to expect perfect love by simple faith, and consequently to expect it now' (*Letters*, Vol.7, p.267). But to his brother Charles in another occasion, 'Go on, in your way, what God has peculiarly called you to...Press the instantaneous blessing: then I shall have more time for my peculiar calling, enforcing the gradual work' (*Letters*, Vol.5, p.16).

The work of sanctifying grace is a dynamic relationship with God in which there are moments of disclosure and realisation and other times of development and growth. Ephesians has the same notion about a dynamic life of the Spirit: That we should 'be being filled' (a continuous flow is assumed in this text) with the Holy Spirit (Ephesians 5:18).

What about your own spiritual journey. Have there been moments when you knew God suddenly and particularly close, transforming your life, as well as times of slow and steady development and growth?

The Resources of Sanctifying Grace

There are two factors which empower our Christian lives and they are intertwined. First the relationship with God, and second our openness to the empowering, equipping and enabling of the Holy Spirit.

- Sanctifying grace assumes we are in a right relationship with God, that we are 'grafted' into Christ, the vine (John 15:1-17).
- That we know, as Wesley knew, that we are pardoned and have peace with God (Romans 5:1-11).
- Sanctifying grace 'perfects' – makes us fit for God's purpose in life.
- Sanctifying grace gives us power for witness (2 Corinthians 4:5 and 7; Acts 1:8).
- Sanctifying grace is a dynamic process – we need to keep on being filled with God's love, with the power of the Holy Spirit ('be being filled' Ephesians 5:18).
- Charles Wesley understood sanctification to be a process. In his hymn, *Love Divine*, he has the image of being 'changed from glory into glory' as God changes our lives. It mirrors Paul's thought in 2 Corinthians 3:18.

Does Sanctifying Grace have limits?

If sanctifying grace is at work in our lives making us more like Jesus, shaping in us Christian perfection – then are there limits? Well, yes, we do not become God, though the divine life of God is alive in us. Think of these:

Our perfection is:

not absolute (God's perfection is unequalled),

not sinless (only Jesus was without sin),

not infallible (not free from ignorance or mistakes to which no blame is attached),

not free from temptation (even Jesus was tempted),

not final (there is always room for growth),

it is not inviolable (it can be lost).

There is a sense in which we are speaking about a perfection which is not perfect. It remains true for all of us that 'God has not finished with me yet!' Christian spirituality is a dynamic relationship, always developing, always with room for growth. Therefore, all consideration of sanctifying grace should be tempered with humility. Thus, Wesley explained, 'Therefore, *sinless perfection* is a phrase I never use' (*A Plain Account of Christian Perfection*, Epworth, 1952, p.45). It is God by his Holy Spirit who is doing the sanctifying and it is by God's mercy that we are transformed. It is not a medal we earn!

Wesley considered the Christian who was open to sanctifying grace was a person 'filled with the love of God' which led to, 'a recovery of the divine nature; the renewal of our souls after the image of God, in righteousness and true holiness.' (*Farther Appeal to Men of Reason and Religion*, 1748).

I find that people can grasp that God's sanctifying grace may be able to shape their lives, and also long for such grace to be active in their lives. What confuses people is that such grace can have anything to do with what Wesley calls 'perfection'. But remember his focus is on the 'perfect love' of God at work in the lives of the Christian person. What then is 'perfect' is God who through the love of the Father, the grace of Jesus and the enabling of the Holy Spirit is at work in our lives. If anything about us is 'perfect' it is the presence of God restoring and shaping our attitudes, values, relationships and behaviour. It is to that shaping which we turn in the next chapter of this study.

Charles Wesley wrote many hymns about sanctification including these verses:

> **Give me a new, a perfect heart,**
> free from all doubt and fear at last;
> the mind which was in Christ impart,
> and let my spirit hold you fast.
>
> O that I now, from sin released,
> your Word may to the utmost prove,
> enter into the promised rest,
> the Canaan of your perfect love!
>
> Now let me gain perfection's height;
> now let me into nothing fall,
> Be less than nothing in your sight,
> and feel that Christ is all in all.

SHAPED BY GRACE

Shaped by Grace

Rising up from the pavements of Hong Kong, lashed together with plastic ties in a formation of half metre squares, bamboo scaffolding towers up around buildings. It is used in construction because as well as being enormously strong, in typhoons it is flexible, in electric storms it does not conduct negative electricity.

Bamboo is used widely in SE Asia because of its strength and pliability which enables it to be shaped into all kinds of uses. It is built into the framework of homes, woven into walls, used to construct furniture, provide matting and in the kitchen formed into all kinds of plates, cups, cutlery and of course, chop-sticks. In Vietnam there are bicycles and even motorcycles with bamboo frames.

Grace is sometimes considered just to be a spiritual experience, or worse, the subject merely of theological discourse! However, it is firmly rooted in human experience. Indeed, John's gospel makes clear that in Jesus' life grace and truth came and walked on earth (John 1:17). Therefore, in this section we explore the ways in which God's transforming grace shapes our lives and plants us firmly in community.

A New Way of Seeing

The very heart of Wesley's theology about grace was that as Christians we are filled with the transforming love of God. He referred regularly to the 'perfect love' of God which affects every aspect of our lives. Such love challenges and changes us to see the world and those around us in a different light. It is seeing with the lens of caring love.

The international evangelist, Billy Graham, said to those who responded at his meetings that they should look for four changes in their lives:

1. to want to pray to a God who they now realise loves and cares for them,
2. to desire to read the scriptures to find out more about Jesus and what it means to follow him,
3. to share their new found faith with another person in the next 24hrs,
4. that they would see the world in different way.

It is that shaping, that seeing God in our lives and the lives of others which is so vital. It is a dynamic process of being regularly challenged by God as we seek to make sense of God's love in and through us.

Read Matthew 5:1-12, which we know as the Beatitudes, a term which comes from *beati* found in Latin versions of the Bible meaning 'Blessed'. These blessings are like a series of proverbs about attitudes which Jesus commends. His hearers, and we as readers, are left to interpret their meaning.

As you read the passage through ask yourself – what are the attitudes which lead to being 'blessed'? Note how practical they are.

Earthed

John Wesley taught that becoming and growing as a Christian is enabled by God's grace. God invites us into a transforming relationship which shapes our lives as we participate in the means of grace. The 'means of grace' are practices, earthed in our lives, through which God by the Holy Spirit deepens our lived discipleship and which become an expression of God's love in our lives.

In his writing the means of grace have two aspects - 'works of piety' which include the devotional reading of scripture, prayer, fasting, holy communion and fellowship, and 'works of mercy' which encompass compassion and service to others. In the next section we will consider what is meant by works of piety but first we reflect on his understanding of works of mercy. Wesley was keen to show that the Christian life should be rooted in actual, practical and relevant service.

Throughout his life he gave generously to help those in need, established schools, founded orphanages, encouraged groups to serve the poor and visit those in prison. He wrote a book on medicine, *Primitive Physick* (containing simple herbal remedies), which he gave to the poor and sold to the rich! He campaigned against slavery, supported William Wilberforce and urged people to visit those in prison. He preached to people on their way to the gallows urging repentance!

The early Methodists were noted for their commitment to bible study and fellowship while at the same time being actively involved in community issues. These Means of Grace are also vital for a rounded, deepening spirituality. It involves the practical works of mercy in caring for others which in turn bring spiritual depth and growth. When Christians practice the works of mercy in love, their love increases, their character (patience, gentleness, etc) is exercised and improved, and they grow in grace.

In the parable of the sheep and the goats (Matthew 25:31-46), Jesus introduces us to the attitudes and actions which are to be expected by those who are disciples. Focus particularly on verses 34-40. What are the ways in which you can be 'earthed' in your lived discipleship? What could you do to support others and alleviate distress and poverty? Consider the ways in which you can share your faith, serve your community, challenge injustice and care for creation.

Sacred Moments

Discipleship, Wesley knew, was a dynamic process and not just an instantaneous experience which remained constant. Christian faith was a relationship with God in Christ by the power of the Holy Spirit and like any other relationship it needed to be nurtured and developed to be fresh and alive. By 'Works of Piety' he meant being in worship, receiving Holy Communion regularly, engaging in personal and corporate prayer, reading the scriptures and being in fellowship sharing about faith and life.

Over the years the Church has developed ways to assist us in reflecting on our discipleship and to grow as Christian people.

- **Prayer** - is not a time when we come with a shopping list to God – a 'Please give us' list! Prayer is being with God, with the whispered prayers of our hearts. Sometimes we run out of words and can only sigh with longing for the welfare of others, or the need of our own lives.
- **Scriptures** – the simple reading of the scriptures opens up for us the story of God's steadfast love, his justice, mercy and kindness. As we read the scriptures, God speaks to us about ourselves, to challenge and change us, to inform and inspire.
- **Healing and wholeness** – there are special services sometimes described in this way but all worship and corporate prayer times have an aspect of bringing healing and wholeness to people. God wants us to flourish as people and as we enter into fellowship and worship, God is working in our lives. Of course, services of prayer for healing and wholeness with anointing with oil are invariably powerful services.
- **Forgiveness** – Jesus began his ministry announcing the need to repent (John 1:19-34, Mark 1:14-15 etc). Remarkably Jesus entrusted to his disciples the authority to forgive sins (Matthew 16:19; John 20:23). Knowing we are forgiven is a liberating thing – which is why we have

the confession each week in our worship and proclaim God's forgiveness. As forgiven people we also are called to forgive others (Colossians 3:13).

John 15:1-11: This passage contains Jesus' teaching to the disciples about the ministry of 'My father, the gardener'. The gardener will remove the dead wood, and prune the branches so we 'bear much fruit'. The motif is powerful for it indicates we are 'grafted' into the vine, Jesus, and bear fruit by obeying his commands.

- What needs to be pruned in your life, values, attitude, priorities?
- How can spiritual growth be encouraged in your life?

Sacraments

These bring us to the heart of the means of grace.

- **Holy Communion**: To receive the sacrament of Holy Communion is an awesome privilege, a time when our lives come under the scrutiny of God grace. It is a reminder for us of the sacrifice of Jesus; a challenge to us that the love of God in Christ has made a way for us to know mercy and forgiveness, a comfort to us that God will be with us. It gives us sacred moments and space to recall the presence of Jesus with us. Communion reminds us of the real presence of Jesus in and with our lives. It sends us out to live and share God's love in the world.
- **Baptism**: In recent years the Methodists have changed the liturgy for Baptism so that grace is declared first with the affirmation of faith, then the baptism and only afterwards the promises. The grace of baptism is dependent on God, not on our promises. Baptism announces God's care for us 'All this for you!' and its

waters are for cleansing. We are sealed with God's love and welcomed into the Christian community.

- **Confirmation** is the time that we testify with humble confidence that the grace of God is alive in our lives and commit ourselves to serve God in the church and the world.

In the new community of God's people there are new values, attitudes, behaviour and relationships. These lead to new actions and priorities. In Acts 2 at the end of Peter's sermon at Pentecost we see the consequences of faith in Jesus. There are things people are asked to do as a response (2:38) and the community of believers is built up as a result.

Acts 2:42-47 describes a Christian community of people who share many things. Think of the church you attend:

- How connected do you feel to others?
- What can you contribute to the life of your Christian community?
- How can the different gifts God has given your church be celebrated?

Engaged

The wonderful truth about the incarnation is that God in Christ comes to be one of us and one with us. It is this attitude of service which is compelling in Jesus' care for others which we see in the gospels. His care for Peter's mother-in-law (Mark 1:29-31), for the marginalised (Luke 18:35-43), reveal Jesus' desire to be engaged with the needy and serve those in need.

Serving the church community. God calls us to leadership roles in the life of the church. God does not call us in order to fill our time or lay burdens on us, but so we can have the privilege and opportunity of serving others in and through the church. We need to be looking for the call of God on our lives to serve Christ in the church and world.

Serving may mean a call to ordained ministry. Wesley spoke of people who had what he termed, an 'extraordinary call'. He saw this in both men and women whom he appointed to preach and then in some whom he called 'helpers' and who today we know as people ordained to a ministry of word and sacrament.

Christian ministry is not a professional trajectory that people embark upon. It is a call of God, insistent and unavoidable, which keeps prompting the person to offer themselves in the service of the church. This of course needs to be tested out by the church, both locally and nationally.

Engaged in community. As the early church worked out the implications of following Jesus they looked wider than the Christian community. James teaches, 'Religion that is pure and undefiled before God, the fathcr, is this: to care for orphans and widows in their distress' (James 1:27).

Justice. We are familiar with texts from Amos 5:24 and Micah 6.8 in which the prophets speak of justice. In the New Testament the issue of justice is partially hidden from us because the Greek word δικαιωσυνη (dikiaōsunē), is normally translated 'righteousness' rather than 'justice' though it carries both meanings. For instance, when we read 2 Peter 3:13 which translates the word as 'righteousness' we imagine that what will be 'at home' are attitudes and practices which are spiritual, but if we translate it as, 'we wait for new heavens and a new earth where *justice* is at home' it carries a different meaning.

Similarly, as Paul summaries his teaching to his readers in Romans 14:17, we can translate it as, 'For the kingdom of God is not food and drink but *justice* and peace and joy in the Holy Spirit'. If we take this reading then justice is part of our message and ministry.

Justice then becomes part of our response to God's grace as disciples which includes a desire to care and speak out about, issues of political transparency, homelessness, care of the poor and disadvantaged.

Justice also means caring for God's creation as a natural response to this gospel of grace. Television programmes such as 'Blue Planet II' (BBC), illustrated for us the environmental crisis and the need for lifestyle change. The 2019 United Nations report on biodiversity and ecosystems has highlighted how fragile our shared environment is. Christians want to rejoice with the Psalmist, 'the earth is the Lord's and all that is in it' (Psalm 24:1). Therefore, we need to be good stewards of creation.

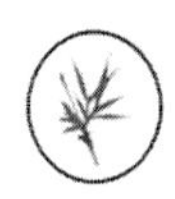

What lifestyle changes can I make to care for creation? Do I recycle, reuse and avoid waste? Are there ways I can join with others to support better use of the earth's resources? What can I do, with others, to bring these things to the attention of policy makers?

Grace at Work in Us!

When writing about the effect of salvation on the inner character of the believer Wesley used the term 'Holy Tempers' to describe the innermost response to the love of God. Wesley was convinced it was the love of God which brings about sanctification. The perfect love of God, alive in the believer, flowing to every part of our lives, transforming values, attitudes, behaviour and relationships.

It is a dynamic process of a relationship with God, Father, Son and Spirit. One in which we are constantly being challenged and equipped by the presence of the God in our lives. As Paul prayed – may we, 'be being filled with the Holy Spirit' Ephesians 5:18.

Therefore, Wesley focussed on the inner character of a person (what he refers to as 'Holy Tempers') before highlighting the outward effect in terms of works of piety and mercy. He sets this out clearly in his sermon *On Zeal*.

In a Christian believer love sits upon the throne which is erected in the inmost soul; namely, love of God and man, which fills the whole heart, and reigns without a rival. In a circle near the throne are all holy tempers; - longsuffering, gentleness, meekness, fidelity, temperance; and if any other were comprised in 'the mind which was in Christ Jesus.' In an exterior circle are all the works of mercy, whether to the souls or bodies of men. By these we exercise all holy tempers- by these we continually improve them, so that all these are real means of grace, although this is not commonly adverted to. Next to these are those that are usually termed works of piety - reading and hearing the word, public, family, private prayer, receiving the Lord's supper, fasting or abstinence. Lastly, that his followers may the more effectually provoke one another to love, holy tempers, and good works, our blessed Lord has united them together in one body, the church, dispersed all over the earth- a little emblem of which, of the church universal, we have in every particular Christian congregation.

Works 7 p.60 Sermon 92 On Zeal

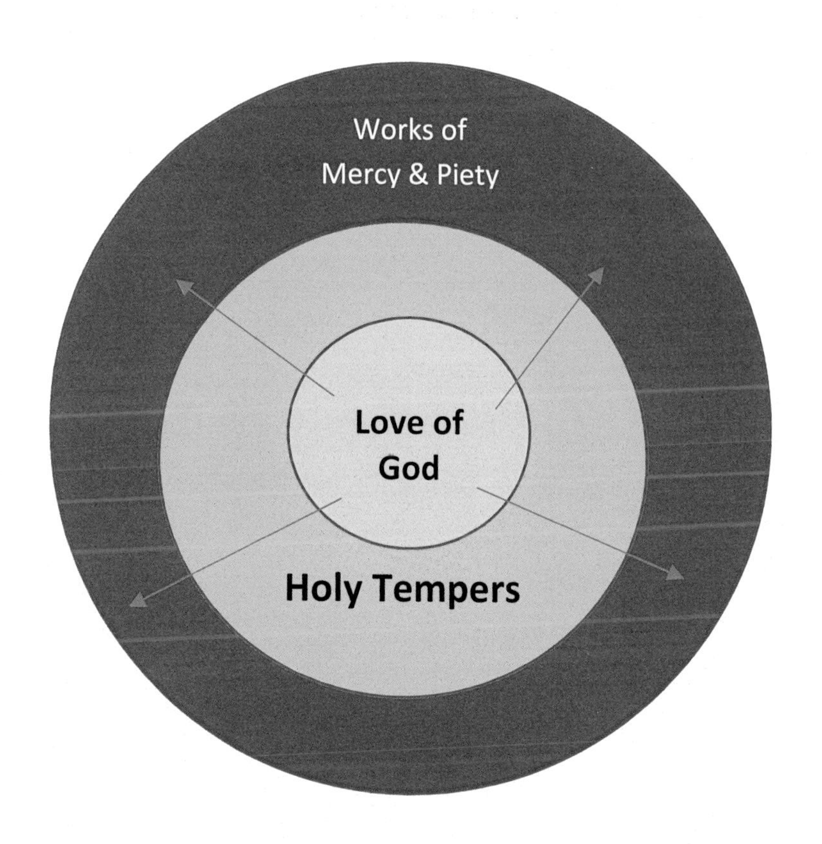

I have set out Wesley's description in the form of a diagram to clarify visually the illustration he gives.

Draw your own diagram of what your faith means to you, of the way God affects your life:

- Where do you place the love of God?
- What are in the circles around it?
- Are they describing your intentions and values – or the things you are doing?
- Does anything need to change?

Grace in All and for All

The means of grace do have a profound influence on our lives – but it is not just for our benefit – always the purpose of God is that we are changed so that we may be a witness, a light, a beacon for others. Such shaping, prompted by the Holy Spirit, enables a deepening spirituality, the transformation of our lives and an outward change towards others.

If I am to live a grace-filled life, and in response to these studies, what action should I take in:

- sharing faith,
- caring for community,
- standing for justice and
- caring for creation

Key Bible verses

Amos 5:24

Let Justice roll down like waters and righteousness like an ever-flowing stream.

Micah 6:8

He (God) has told you, O mortal, what is good: and what does the Lord require of you but to do justice, and to love kindness, and to walk humbly with your God?

1 John 4:10-12

In this is love, not that we loved God but that he loved us and sent his Son to be the atoning sacrifice for our sins. Beloved, since God loved us so much, we also ought to love one another.

No one has ever seen God; if we love one another, God lives in us, and his love is perfected in us.

Luke 9:23

If any want to become my followers, let them deny themselves and take up their cross and follow me.

This famous hymn by Charles Wesley captures the joy of living in the perfect love of God.

Love divine, all loves excelling,
joy of heaven to earth come down,
fix in us thy humble dwelling,
all thy faithful mercies crown.
Jesu, thou art all compassion,
pure unbounded love Thou art;
visit us with thy salvation,
enter every trembling heart.

Come, almighty to deliver,
let us all thy life receive;
suddenly return, and never,
never more thy temples leave.
Thee we would be always blessing,
serve thee as thy hosts above,
pray and praise thee, without ceasing,
glory in thy perfect love.

Finish then thy new creation,
pure and spotless let us be;
let us see thy great salvation,
perfectly restored in thee:
changed from glory into glory,
till in heaven we take our place,
till we cast our crowns before thee,
lost in wonder, love, and praise! Charles Wesley

A Prayer

Come Holy Spirit,
shape us in your love,
enable us by your power,
equip us by your grace.
Form the character of Christ within us,
establish the ministry of Christ through us,
that with dynamic kindness
lives may be transformed,
creation and community renewed,
to be something beautiful for God.

Commendations

In a winsome and accessible way, Howard Mellor introduces some of the central themes of Christian faith. Written from a Wesleyan and Methodist perspective, and drawing upon insights from ministry in a number of different cultures, *Embracing Grace* will be a blessing to all Christians, using to great effect reflection, study and group material which will encourage and deepen your discipleship of Christ.

Revd Dr Martyn Atkins, Superintendent Minister, Methodist Central Hall, Westminster

It is not at all surprising to me that Howard's many skills and the breadth of his experience have come together to offer such a rounded encounter with grace. It is an encounter grounded in scripture, reason tradition and experience, encircled by prayer and including the challenge to respond.

It is particularly good that it invites response in so many different ways. It is very positively interactive but grounded in a depth of theology and biblical understanding. This is a rich resource for all of us who are followers of Jesus seeking to respond to the gracious call of God.

Revd Ruth Gee, Assistant Secretary of the Methodist Conference

'Grace' might be a small word but it is at the very heart of Christian faith, and in these studies Howard Mellor invites us to delve into its many meanings. It was an especially important theme for the Wesleys, so expect to learn about Methodist history and liturgy as well as delving into scripture. You might even learn a bit of Greek – but most of all, be reminded of the love of God and find encouragement for faithful devotion.

Professor John Drane, Chaplain & Professor of Practical Theology @ UWS Paisley

Biography

Howard has served Methodist Churches in four widely differing circuits: Deptford and Greenwich, Croydon, Winchester and Hong Kong. For twenty-one years he worked at Cliff College in two posts as Director of Evangelism and Principal. Now a Supernumerary Minister living in Winchester, Howard is an Ecumenical Canon at Winchester Cathedral. He is often found in Hong Kong supporting the work of the Methodist International Church and is a visiting lecturer at the Cambodian Methodist Bible School in Phnom Penh. When in the UK he volunteers for the Live at Home Scheme (MHA) as a chef, and the National Trust as a gardener.